A Memoir of
Unspoken Words

Abbie Patrick

A Memoir of Unspoken Words

Copyright © 2024 by Abbie Patrick.

All rights reserved. No part of this publication may be reproduced, distributed, or transmitted in any form or by any means, including photocopying, recording, or other electronic or mechanical methods, without the written consent of the publisher. The only exceptions are for brief quotations included in critical reviews and other noncommercial uses permitted by copyright law.

MILTON & HUGO L.L.C.
4407 Park Ave., Suite 5
Union City, NJ 07087, USA

Website: *www. miltonandhugo.com*
Hotline: *1- 888-778-0033*
Email: *info@miltonandhugo.com*

Ordering Information:
Quantity sales. Special discounts are granted to corporations, associations, and other organizations. For more information on these discounts, please reach out to the publisher using the contact information provided above.

Library of Congress Control Number:	2024916294
ISBN-13: 979-8-89285-259-3	[Paperback Edition]
979-8-89285-261-6	[Hardback Edition]
979-8-89285-260-9	[Digital Edition]

Rev. date: 07/17/2024

Dedication

This book is dedicated to my loving husband, who has made countless sacrifices to make this book possible. His encouragement and endless support have aided in the creation and quality. I also want to thank my cat, Meeka, for the constant cuddles and love on days I have spent writing. This book was created for anyone struggling with their mental health, traumatic life events, or misfortunes. I hope this book brings you peace and you find that you are not alone. So many people struggle every day, and I wanted to shed light to those people and how those dark moments can feel. I love you, reader, and hope this collection of poems finds you well.

Trigger Warning:
There are mentions of self-harm, eating disorders, abuse, sexual assault, suicidal ideation, as well as other mental illnesses in the pages ahead. Be gentle to yourself and read with care.

Hauntings of the Night

I lay still,
Sunken into my bed.

Wrapped in a cocoon of pillows and blankets.

They surround me,
Keeping me safe with their inevitable barrier.

So heavy over top of me,
I couldn't move if I tried.

My mind is wide awake,
Almost nocturnal at this point.

My eyes shift toward my almost shut bedroom door.
A dim light makes its presence known,
Peaking between the cracks.

The light is kind to my eyes,
But the voices travelling through it,
Are harsh to my mind.

I jolt up in bed,
My adrenaline pumping a mile a second.

Staying quiet is my only objective.

Their harsh words,
Along with the sound of objects
Carelessly being thrown,
Are all I know
About nighttime.

I stay hugging the door
That separates me from the monsters.

Their violent words grow
Louder

And
Louder
And
Louder

Until
...
Silence.

I act swiftly.
In one perfect motion I enter the room of beasts.

"mommy?"
"daddy?"
"where did the monsters go?"

Peace Amongst the Chaos

Everyday
Was different.

Different expectations.
Different passing ons of guilt.
Different violent terms.
Different consequences to pay.
Different "Forms of Love".

My self-doubt
Remained the only constant.

The only thing I could control,
Was how I achieved peace:

Perfection.

It's difficult to find solitude,
Through someone who's next move
Was a constant game of chess.

To my dismay,
I didn't know how to play.

For a while I tried to play your game.

Until that moment came
when I prioritized loving myself,
Instead of chasing gratification

From someone who couldn't be pleased
behind closed doors.

To this day,
I keep my door opened.

Childhood Misfortune

That poor young girl
Would rather:

Get splinters in both feet

Be stung by a Bee

Burn her feet on hot pavement

Wreck her tricycle

Trip over her toys

Skin her knees

Fall out of bed

Brush tangles out of her hair

Fall off the swing

Than feel your harsh words
Wrap around her like barbed wire.

Cutting into her innocence
Her happiness
Her youth.

Demolish the Old, Create the New

>   Building walls
>   And setting boundaries
>   Are two completely different things.
>   Destroy your walls.
>   You are just as safe
>   Behind a boundary.

Childhood Profession

I always thought of you fondly.
As a superhero.
A perfect human
In all your essence.

I had a firm belief
Of what your role was meant to be
In my life.

But I became that role.

I was your protector.
Your peacemaker.
Your strongest defense.
Your personal advocator.

Silent when I needed to be.
Strong when you asked me to be.
Willful when you wanted me to be.

The energy
So strong
I often knew without a word,
What I needed to do.
Who I needed to be.

I was 10 years old.

You do the Math

                              20 times
                        Or they'll drown.
            1 pass on each hand with the soap
                              20 times
                     Or my family will drown.

                             "Dinner!!!!"
                            My mom yells.

            I sit down in my chair at the table,
                  Adjusting my Care Bears placemat
                   To line the edge of the table
                              Perfectly.

                     I pick up my glass of water,
                           And drink slowly.
                            I set it down,
                              Pick it up.
                             Set it down,
                              Pick it up.
                             Set it down,
                              Pick it up.

                    "Why doesn't it FEEL right."

        After dinner I make my way to the T.V. room.

                 I have to turn the volume from 0
                                To 20
                          7 times in a row
                              Perfectly.
                         Or I must restart.

                  I was too young to understand
        That this would be the beginning of a lifelong
                                battle.
        Too young to understand that this unnerving feeling
                          Of restlessness,

Is the first instance of anxiety in my life.
Too young to understand
That it's consuming me.

Everywhere I go
Everything I do
Must feel right
Sound right
Be.
Right.

It's either this
Or death and devastation.
And every time,
I chose to be the savior.

Composition of my Being

Lies.

I'm an award-winning actress.
The camera pans to my face
And I confidently lie.
I proudly,
Lie.

Torcher.

I scrub over the marks on my skin,
Wiping myself clean of your touch.
The soap stinging just enough to make my eyes water,
You harm me without being present.

Silence.

My mouth is sewn shut.
I couldn't ask for help-
For mercy
Even if I wanted to.
Suffocating in the pain,
Your
"love"
In the silence.

Resilience

Miraculously, I still stand.
My feet remain burrowed in the ground beneath me.
I pray for the day I finally fall.
But my body has a mind of its own,
A prayer of its own.

It Lurks

"Now I lay me down to sleep,
I pray the lord my soul to keep.
And if I die before I wake"
. . .

Tighter,
I close my eyes tighter than ever.

My brain craves a deep slumber,
Yet is terrified to try.

What IS sleep?
Analyzing the process of falling into darkness,
I AM TERRIFIED.

The thought of closing my eyes,
No.
Shutting my mind off...
Is petrifying.

Shadows begin to form in the darkness that surrounds me.

They remain a safe distance away,
Watching me.
Always.
Watching.

They mock my failed attempts at peace.

It's like my body has an instinct,
A warning of sorts,
That I am not safe in such a vulnerable state.

So I stay awake.
Up until I pass out from complete and total exhaustion.
Up until,
I become a shadow in itself.

Stalked

						It started out
					As a casual run in at work.

				You always requested my help
					And I always gave it.

						Every time I saw you,
					You seemed so friendly.
							So honest.

						Until the moment,
					My open drink fizzed
						As you walked past.

					In the days to follow,
				You would ask for my number,
					Knowing I was a minor.

			Tell me my cars make and model.

	Write the code that was my license plate
					One a piece of paper,
						And slip it to me
					Subtly over the counter.

					Hide in the parking lot,
						Trying to scare me.

					Tape pictures of children
				On the pavement beside my car.

                    Shove phony notes
            Under my windshield wipers.

                    You would follow me home.

                    I'm only just now able

                            To drive my car
            Without checking my backseat.

Teenage Testimony

They swarm like mosquitos.
Sucking the life out of you,
Rapidly and viciously.
A constant competition for a title that doesn't matter.
What you wear,
What you LOOK like,
Your wealth,
You're friends,
Your brand.
It matters to them
Too much.
They seek perfection
Everywhere but within.
And you will always fall short.
Their pathetic attempt to
Morph you,
Convincing you that you're
Worth changing.
It's all a ridiculously played game.
And you will always lose.

Friendly Reminder to Myself

Life has given me
The most beautiful amount of peace
Now that I don't
Have friends.

No more strain in effort.
A lack of wasted energy.

Beautifully myself,
The quiet solitude
Is nothing but accepting.

Nothing but calm.

Trust Me, I Can Swim

They say you sink or swim.
If this is the case
I must have been born into a pool of water
Lacking the basic instinct, I needed to survive.
At first it was welcoming.
It held me in an embrace like none I've ever felt.
Surrounded by the cool undertones I rejoiced in how freely my
Limbs could move.
I was gifted to the water.
Nonetheless it wasn't long before my thoughts submerged me more than the tide ever could.
With each stroke forward I find myself sinking a few more inches.
The waves now fierce and vigorous.
1 step forward, 3 steps back.
I still find comfort in the water as it fills my lungs.
Each breath presumptuously my last.
I do not fear the water, as vast and as deep as it may be.
To my dismay, I like the water.
I am safe in the water.
I am okay with this.

Stop, Drop, Roll.

It's 12 AM.
I toss and turn with the television light
Illuminating the skin on my face.

Everything is calm
Except my mind.

And thus it begins.

A single drop of sweat quickly rolls down my cheek.
I am hot.
It is hot in here.

I thrash around,
Shoving all my blankets to the floor.
Stripping myself of all my clothes.

My skin pours sweat
Like a fountain of doom.

The rise and fall in my chest grows shallow,
Rapid,
Uneven.

My body begins to tremble violently.
A quick reaction to the heat.
To the fear.

The nerves in my abdomen burn with a recklessness
That leaves me on my knees.

My vision,
As black as soot,
Are met with an explosive ringing in my ears.

My face begins to tingle as I attempt to shout for help.

My words are but a mere whisper,
In the smoke-filled air.

The fire growing in my mind and body,
Tampers my soul.
Aches my heart.
Scares my lungs.

I lay silently.
Sparks from the fire singe my skin.
A subtle reminder that how I feel is real.

I Need a Bandaid

You treated me like a chapter,
Yet I read you like a novel.
Written so elegantly,
Your words left your lips with a bittersweet touch.
I was eager to learn more,
To uncover everything your story offered.
It was my favorite past time,
Reading you, studying you.
I was in complete awe of each and every line.
It reminded me of my favorite season,
Autumn,
Your story did.
The vibrant colors, the festivities, the perfect chill covering a warm breeze.
But the lack of foreshadowing for the cold dark months ahead left me reading blindly.
Despite all my intellect,
You glazed over my chapter and sat my book back on the shelf.
It remained dusty and untouched.
Your words quickly turned cold,
Like a lonely January evening.
With every page turn I get a papercut.
It hurts.
Don't you see?
I'm hurting.
You're hurting me.
If you would pick up my book and scan the pages
You would recognize that.
Am I boring you?
Are my pages not worthy?
Don't you want to know who I am?
...
I finished your novel.
I returned it to you.
I won't ask to borrow it again.

Message in a Bottle

Never let someone convince you that
Your expectations are too high.
However,
Don't create expectations
Out of the fear of being hurt.

10th Grade Spelling Bee

Trust?
Can you give me the definition, please?
Firm belief in the reliability, truth, ability, or strength of someone or something.
Trust.
Can you use it in a sentence?
I shouldn't have trusted you.
Trust.
T-R-U-S-T
Trust.

Morphology

The numbers on the scale are her religion.

Her mind worships its own concept of perfection.

She follows this ideology wholeheartedly.

Count your calories.
Check.
Baggy clothing.
Check.
2-3 fingers down the throat.
Check.
Eat strictly to survive.
Check.
Exercise.
Check.

She may not consciously be aware,
But these are the rules of her religion.

She follows them like her life depends on it.
Why doesn't she look perfect?
She's losing weight but not enough.
Why isn't it working?

She's subconsciously obsessed.
She wants to be freed,
But it's harder to be free than it is to be perfect.

. . .

You are beautiful.
You are perfect.
In all your essence,
You are worthy of self-love.

Starving Statements

"I'm not hungry."
"I already ate."
"I don't like that kind of food."
"I didn't have time."
"I forgot."
"I get full so fast."
"I'm eating later."

She was so good at her game
It almost cost her
Her life.

The Looking Glass

                    I pray for the day
                    You see in yourself
                       Who the girl
        On the inside of the mirror
                           Truly is.

Timeline Tragedy

I met you.
I liked you.
I wanted you.
I loved you.
I needed you.
I yearned for you.
I was hurt by you.
We fought.
We made up.
We fought.
I compromised.
We fought.
I gave in.
We fought.
I was tired.
You grew distant.
You neglected us.
I cried.
I was angry.
I stopped caring.
You came back.
I pretended.
You were happy.
I was numb.
We separated.
I missed you.
You moved on.
We broke up.
I was happy.
I was myself.
You missed me.
You came back.
I rejected you.
We parted ways.
We blocked numbers.
We deleted pictures.
We became individuals.

The Person You Are Trying to Reach Has a Voicemail Box That Has Not Been Set up Yet

"hey,
It's me.
There are just some things I need to get off my chest.
The last time we spoke, I saw right through you.
You only missed having me because I'm doing so good without you.
I have never felt freer,
More myself,
HAPPIER,
Than when we ended things.
You far too often put yourself on a false pedestal above me.
You mocked my mental struggles,
You lied to me, manipulated my trust, went behind my back.
-a piece of advice:
Don't date an emotional person
If you know you're emotionally unavailable.
Do you know how hard it is to fight with someone,
Who doesn't care about you OR the problem?
I'm honestly ashamed I was ever with you.
The thought of you now disgusts me.
Who you are
Disgusts me.
I deserved so much more, and so much better
During such a crucial and pivotal time in my life.
You neglected that.
You neglected me.
I am free from your actions,
Your words,
Your mind.
And I've never been happier.

P.S.
Block my number after listening to this."

Acceptance

>He doesn't need to love you
> For you to love yourself.

Homesick Farewells

Your joy.
Your Honesty.
Your Kindness.
Your love.
You.
I miss you.
In an ever-evolving world,
You were the constant.
My heart aches knowing I can't call.
Knowing I can't hug you.
I hope you never had to question my love for you.
That I made you proud.
That you saw yourself,
Your kindness,
Shine through my heart.
I hope you were met with peace.
I feel you,
With me always.
Your hand on my shoulder,
Guiding me.
Please,
Never let go.

Rewinding the Clock

There is no greater feeling of regret
Than after mourning the loss of someone
Special enough
To make you question
How you've spent
The time in your life.

The Ghost inside the Girl

I see the world through a lens.

Watching myself
From above.
From a different perspective.

"Shit."
"Am I still high?"

I will ask myself this question everyday
For 5 months.

I no longer recognize who I see in the mirror,
Staring blankly back at me.

I stopped taking my meds.
All I want is to feel something.
Anything.
To prove I'm real.
To prove that
This
Is real.

The smallest of sensations now overstimulates me.
Only a small part of me feels them.

There's only one logical explanation:
"I'm in a coma"

Everything feels like a dream.
Yes.
That must be it.

I confide in others how I'm feeling,
Only to be tossed aside.

"do they think I'm joking?"
"did they hear me?"
"wait. Did I imagine telling them?"

I guess people only care when you're dead or dying.

What they don't know is I'm already dead inside.

The Stars on Her Sleeve

She was never sure why she did it.
Like a compulsion accompanied without thoughts.
She just knew she had to.

She could hide them easily.
Until she couldn't.

It was always an "accident".

A mishap while shaving.
A scratch from her pet.
A burn from the stove.

She felt guilty about them.
But guilt was met with self-punishment.

Like the water cycle,
It was a never-ending sequence.

Her bathroom door hid more than red bath water and salty tears.

Her trashcan concealed more than bandaid scraps and their accompanying tools.

Her eyes though,
Gave it all away.

The Secret in my Medicine Cabinet

A pill a day.
One measly pill.
The "20 milligrams" written on the face of the
bottle taunts me every time I twist the cap.
Don't get me wrong,
I'm not ashamed of it.
Clearly,
or I wouldn't be telling you this about me.
Disregarding what this pill is capable of,
I find myself asking the same question every day.
Why should I take the world so seriously when I
rely on a pill to be happy?
The narcissistic thing about it is,
I'm just now opening my mind enough to realize,
I'm not the only person wondering the answer to
that question.

Music for my blackened heart

I always knew I was depressed,
When I focused on the meaning
Instead of the instruments.

I always knew I was numb,
When I could no longer hear
Anything being played.

I Can Rhyme

In the pillows and blankets
That compose her bed,
That once willful girl
Now lays dead.

The ongoing guilt and shame
From her effortless
lifestyle,
Can't be tamed.

Too exhausted
To try to stand,
The depression now has
The upperhand.

She lays in a puddle
Of her own tears.
And reminisces
of better years.

Highway Hypnosis

There is nothing
Quite like
Arriving at your destination
With no idea how you got there.

No remembrance of anything
You passed on the road.

A complete Disassociated state of mind,
To drown out everything
That appears
Through the windows of your car.

Nevertheless,
You always reach
Where you're trying to go.

I Hope the Guilt Seeks You Out

Do you think of yourself as a good person?

Even after how your coarse hands touched my skin?

Even after all the phone calls to "chit chat"?

After startling me awake in the middle of the night,
While your daughter slept peacefully beside me?

For telling me I couldn't sleep with my friend on vacation with your family?
Knowing I didn't feel safe?

For grazing my legs and lower back in the pool?

For staring a little too long at my appearance?

For touching me anytime you saw me?

For lying about your motives?

. . .

I was 15.

Morals of the Wretched

I was blackout drunk.
I said
"no".
But even if
I agreed,
You had no business
Performing the acts
Against me
That you did.
Your sobriety
Knew the state of my mind.
You shouldn't have even asked.
You shouldn't have encouraged
The criminal acts
You were desiring.
You had nothing to lose,
Yet I lost everything.
I was just another notch on your belt.
A statistic.
An object.

A Needed Cleanse

>No amount of soap
Can prevent me from feeling dirty
After you touch me.

Catching up With a Friend

Mid book check in, here!
Have you taken your meds?
What about drank some water?
Gotten any fresh air?
Anything you need to get off your chest?
Be gentle with yourself today.
I love you.

Reminiscing Better Days

Growing up I rarely wore shoes to play outside.
Not because I was lazy, or didn't know how to tie them,
But because I liked how the cool pavement felt on the soles of my feet.
I enjoyed the blades of grass slipping between my toes,
Petals of flowers clinging to my skin.
It was a euphoric feeling that reminded me of my youth and innocence.
But as I grew older it was no longer petals and evergreen grass that I was stepping on.
It became rocks,
Bumblebees,
Concrete so hot you'd swear your foot caught fire.
Nonetheless I began to wear shoes,
Not because I wanted to,
But as a form of protection, really.
Each growing year I would lace them tighter and tighter,
Hoping they would keep my feet safe.
When would I remember that not everything I step on will inflict pain?
When would I realize that belts can come undone without the motive of sex?
That hands can graze my skin without leaving a red mark,
That I can be spoken to without being belittled,
That not every person I encounter is a questionable character.
I miss my innocence.
I miss feeling protected.
Maybe tomorrow I won't wear my shoes.

Possessed

everyone has demons.
sometHing inside of them that torments
and teases their happinEss.

I always preferred to think that my demons
would enable rebeLlion and good times,
to my dismay, they leave me stuck in bed,
Pulling my hair out.

What a joke.
Right?

I wish my psychiatrist could perform an exorcisM.

If I ever tried to tell her that,
i'm sure she'd up my mEds.

It doesn't make the feeling any less real,
though.

I have come to accept them,
the demons.

They still scare me,
but I digress.

Coin Toss

"She's sleeping too much."
"She never sleeps."

"She's eating too much."
"She hardly eats."

"She was very outspoken today."
"She barely said a word."

"She seemed on edge."
"She is careless."

"She put too much effort in today."
"She doesn't put any effort into herself."

"She is so irritable."
"She seems too happy."

"She isn't productive."
"She's trying to do too much."

What will they say about me tomorrow?

Individualism

You're only proud of me
When my accomplishments match
Your idea of who I should be.

Freedom

"Who are you idealizing
To dress like that?
Look like that?
Be like that?"

Myself.

Spaced is The Mind

Her mind
In a hypnotic state of silence.

Vision blurry,
Muted surroundings,
Her body frozen in time.

For those brief moments of peace,
She thinks of nothing.
She feels nothing.
She is
Nothing.

She tries to come back
To reality.
But the control center
That is her mind
Doesn't acknowledge her efforts.

This is one thing in life,
She is okay
With not being able
To control.

Homeostasis

            The skin on her fingers
            Have been peeled away.

        Her eyebrows and eyelashes
                    Are sparse.

        Her hair covers the scabs
                    On her scalp.

        Her fingernails are thin
        And sharpened by her teeth.

    She is in a state of relaxation.

Double Edged Sword

>If her anxiety wasn't so bad
>She probably wouldn't fear
>The unknown
>Of death

Identify

Who am i?

In a society undergoing constant evolution,
I'm never caught up.

I don't watch the news,
The far too biased opinions,
Meshed with impending doom,
Steers me away.

I don't follow social norms.
They trap me in a box.

Hell,
The constant change in beauty standards
Is too much for even a model to follow.

Let us not forget,
Societies unreasonable expectations that
Are set to be unachievable.

Meanwhile,
Social media is the new addictive distraction,
Used to escape.

All things considered,
Where do I stand amongst this.
Who AM I?

I never know.

Yes.
I'm a good person.
Yes.
I have aspirations.
Yes.
I have a life plan.
Yes.

I'm in love.

But,
Who AM I?

My identity is constantly evolving,
Never resting.

It's exhausting trying to compose,
And keep up with
An identity.

I guess that's why I copy yours.

Flourish

Flowers are no longer wilted.

I watch through my still cold kitchen window
At my neighbors,
Tending to their gardens.

This was my first glance at spring.

Joy rushes through me
Like a coffee that's too hot,
Burning my walls as it travels
Down.

"My seasonal blues are in the past.
This is a fresh start."

Or maybe,
They were never seasonal.
I just simply get distracted by
The continuous melancholic
Feelings that consume my chest and stomach,
Whenever winters says its farewell.

Flowers.

The rich colors that blossom from
The vibrant green stems.
Very harmonic but only when you
Give them the proper nurturing.

Flowers are the kinds of people i
Seek to attract
In my lifetime.

People who blossom still yet
After the injustice of a cold winter.

People who are willful

And prepare for the next chapters in
Their lives.

People who are beautiful.

People who let their neon energy
Project onto me.

People who need me to breathe life
Back into them,
Just as they breathe life back
Into me.

Good
P E O P L E.

Mirror's Image

You followed me to the bathroom,
Granted, I didn't ask for your company-
But you knew I needed it.
You always knew what I needed.
You knew me better than I knew myself.
I didn't want to see the wreck that I was through the mirror,
So, you held me in the dark.
You whispered kind words to me.
If my heart wasn't beating so loud maybe I would have heard them.
Eyes puffy and my nose running, you cleaned me up.
Gentle.
Is the only way I can describe your touch.
The light flickers on.
I look brand new.

Safe Spaces for the Lonely

The mossy ground
Wraps its cold arms around my legs.

The smell of rain in the distance
Floods my nose.
As I breathe,
Deeper

And deeper

And deeper.

I stare deeply upward.
The trees,
A dark emerald green,
Covering my field of vision.

Every now and then,
A drop of water will splash my face.
The cold subtle sensation brings me peace.

My palms lay on a bed of pine needles
On either side of me.

I stare intently at the wildlife
That hovers protectively around me.

Bears,
Moose,
Squirrels,
Rabbits,
Foxes,
Eagles.

They carefully and lovingly
Surround me.

In a perfect circle,

Engulfing the forest,
Is a brick wall.

Perfect solitude.
No one can enter.

Except you.

If I'm Being Honest

I see you,
Trying to comfort me,
Trying to be present.
You made a mistake.
You could feel it in your heart.
Am I too stubborn to let my emotions aside, just enough for you to be there for me?
It's deeper than that.
I've come to terms with the fact that I'm more upset with myself, than I am by the pain you've inflicted.
I'm the issue.
I do apologize for the game of tug of war I've been playing with you.
I can't decide whether to pull you closer or to push you away
Anytime I feel something other than happiness.
But either way we both lose.
There is no winner to this game I have created.
Not because you made a mistake,
But because I've yet to learn how to handle the aftermath.

Tales For a Lonely Heart

Never dismiss the love of others
During moments of emotional weakness.
Rather,
Shift your mind to the idea
That you deserve to be loved

Quiet Mouse

I lay in our bed with the darkness consuming me.
My tears have formed a puddle on my pillowcase.
Mountains of tissues are the only barrier between us,
As you stand over me,
Feeling just as hopeless as I do in this moment of solitude.
Why?
Why.
You made a mistake.
Because of that we both suffer.
My head is swarmed with questions that you don't have the answers to.
Why?
Why.
My body feels as though it's been torn in two.
Tunnel vision prevents me from seeing real life.
The trash can beside me is prepared enough for me to throw up my heart.
I have no words.
Why?
Why.
But it wasn't you.
You performed nothing against me.
Your testimony to us remains true, as you promised all those times before.
They just want me to believe them.
The voices.
That you've committed disrespectful acts towards our love.
Why?

Why can't I understand it's not real.
None of this is real.
Just figments of my darkest imagination.
The voices grow louder as my doubt increases.
I am coming to my senses.
Make them stop!
Please.
PLEASE!
MAKE THEM SHUT UP!
"1-2-3 Quiet Mouse".

Tales of Heartache

                              The concept of "Love"
                              Was always knew to her.

                                    She would learn
                                  Time and time again

                                    What Love wasn't.

Underrated Companion

The day I got you
Was destiny played out.
So soft,
So innocent,
So perfect.
The moment your kind eyes locked with mine,
I fell in love.
A love I had never felt before,
But was eager to deepen.
Small enough to fit in my hand,
I held you tenderly.
Although I mother you, meet your needs, ensure your happiness,
What you do for me,
Could never be repaid.
You save me.
Everyday.
The love you give me
Is too often than not
All I ever need.
I feel at home with you.
Your soul speaks to me kind words of encouragement.
Your love overwhelms me.
Your touch puts me into a deep state of peace.
I carry you in my heart,
Everywhere I go.
Your precious face
Is the most beautiful I've ever seen.
You are my perfect ball of fur.

My Mistress- Nostalgia

Everywhere I go,
I am followed by a young girl.

Her Wide eyes always glaring up at me.
She admires me.
She loves me.

With every bad thought I have about myself,
She looks at me,
Her eyes filled with tears.

Every time I haven't shown myself love,
Her heart breaks
More and more.

I have tried endlessly,
To preserve her innocence.
To give her the happiness she deserves.
To be gentle,
Caring,
Soft spoken.

That's always all she needs.

I mother her.
I let her vicariously live through me.
Shamelessly.

That little girl is me.

My Mistress- Empowerment

Empowerment is an important concept
For girls to understand.

I have always known I was the black sheep
Of the family.

My families' beliefs and minds
Don't resonate with me.

I liked to tell myself I was
Special.

In reality, I'd call it
"breaking a cycle".

It is empowering to be different.
To be unique.
To be yourself.

That is the number one lesson,
I have taught my younger self.

No matter what she will encounter,
Her future self will always
Cheer her on.

The sacrifices she makes,
Never go unnoticed
By me.

Reversing the Time

It wasn't until I met you
That I felt comfortable enough to act like a child.
The stuffed animals on my side of the bed,
Appreciate the softness you show me.
The feeling of being vulnerable,
Cared for,
Loved for everything I am.
The feeling of security
From laying on your chest,
Wrapped in my blanket,
Is nothing short of
Holy.
Your soft kisses on my forehead
Make me feel small, innocent, and protected.
Your encouragement of my childlike spirit
Makes my younger self nothing short of happy.
Thank you for giving me
What I needed all those years ago.
Thank you
For letting me have a childhood.

Milton Keynes UK
Ingram Content Group UK Ltd.
UKHW042337121024
449589UK00001B/37